Along New Mexico's Continental Divide Trail

Photography by Tom Till
with William Stone

Text by David Patterson

www.westcliffepublishers.com

Contents

Sunflowers grow in profusion in Red Rock State Park.

International Standard Book Number: 1-56579-346-3
Photography Copyright: Tom Till, 2001. All rights reserved.
                                William Stone, 2001. All rights reserved.
Text and Photography Copyright: David Patterson, 2001. All rights reserved.

Editor: Jenna Samelson
Designers: Craig Keyzer and Carol Pando
Production Manager: Craig Keyzer
Map Designer: Carol Pando

Published By:
Westcliffe Publishers, Inc.
P.O. Box 1261
Englewood, CO 80150
www.westcliffepublishers.com

Printed in Hong Kong through World Print, Ltd.

Library of Congress Cataloging-in-Publication Data:

Patterson, David D. (David Dewitt), 1972-
    Along New Mexico's Continental Divide Trail / photography by Tom Till with William
    Stone ; text by David D. Patterson
        p. cm.
    ISBN 1-56579-346-3
    1. Continental Divide National Scenic Trail--Description and travel. 2. Continental
Divide National Scenic Trail--Pictorial works. 3. New Mexico--Description and travel. 4.
New Mexico--Pictorial works. 5. Patterson, David D. (David Dewitt),
1972---Journeys--Continental Divide National Scenic Trail. 6. Patterson, David D.
(David Dewitt), 1972---Journeys--New Mexico. 7. Hiking--Continental Divide National
Scenic Trail. 8. Hiking--New Mexico. I. Till, Tom. II. Title.
F721 .P38 2001
917.8904'53--dc21   00-020722

*For more information about other fine books and calendars from Westcliffe Publishers, please contact your local bookstore, call us at 1-800-523-3692, write for our free color catalog, or visit us on the Web at **www.westcliffepublishers.com**.*

First frontispiece: *A meadow of Colorado loco blooms in Carson National Forest.*
Second frontispiece: *The Rio Chama at sunset, upstream from Abiquiu Lake.*
Third frontispiece: *Hourglass Arch in Gobernador Canyon.*
Opposite: *A vibrant claret cup cactus in El Malpais National Monument.*

Acknowledgments

I would like to thank everyone who has worked to make the Continental Divide Trail a reality, from those who have physically constructed the trail to the citizens who pushed our government for its creation. John Fielder, photographer and publisher, deserves a great deal of credit for making the public aware of the vast resources this trail and the country it passes through offer. My family, again, put up stoically with my frequent absences. My son once asked, "Dad, are you ever going to stop going to New Mexico?" I appreciate the support and love of Marcy, Mikenna, Bryce, Christina, and Cora. Many thanks to Linda Doyle at Westcliffe Publishers for her good nature and encouragement. Bob Julyan was a great trail companion and gave me a lot of information about where the trail really was, and where it "might be." Thanks also to the public lands agencies, managers, and rangers who oversee the lands surrounding the Continental Divide: the National Park Service, the U.S. Forest Service, and the Bureau of Land Management. Finally, thanks to the many tow truck operators and others who pulled my truck out of the mud.

—Tom Till

I would like to thank Tom Till and the folks at Westcliffe Publishers for welcoming me into this wonderful project. I could not ask for better backcountry adventure partners than my friends Bob Julyan and Jim Shelton. My parents, Helen and Ed Stone of Newport, Rhode Island, have been a tremendous source of support and encouragement through the years. And finally, I thank my wife, Carolyn, for her love, companionship, and patience.

—William Stone

Fall graces a bigtooth maple in the Black Range with fiery hues.

Opposite: *Sunrise illuminates the rugged cliffs of Ghost Ranch.*

Acknowledgments

What many hikers commonly refer to as "Trail Magic" really results from the hard work, patience, and understanding of others. Those who help you on and off the trail somehow relate to your adventure, whether they live vicariously through your experience or are in the midst of their own adventures. In essence there's no real "magic," just the willingness of a human being—a "Trail Angel"—to share your dreams briefly, if not indefinitely. My past few years of thru-hiking wouldn't have been possible without the support of my family—exhausted from constantly mailing my parcels— my friends, and the wonderful people along the way. Thanks to everyone who shared in my successes and helped me pursue my dreams.

Thanks to my parents, Pat and Sandra Patterson; my sisters, Michele and Denise, and my brother, Brian; Karyn Jilk for everything; Larry and Marcia Jilk; Allan Swayze (Campro) for the ride, maps, and friendship; Marty Swayze; Henry Weir (Hasil) *Whooo!*; Andrew Helliwell; C. W. Banfield; special thanks to Caithlin Hull for inviting me to Colorado and hiking with me post–New Mexico; Roger Carpenter and ALDHA–West for my Triple Crown Award; Wayne Gregory and Debbie Morse for providing my Gregory Backpacks;

Bill Homer for providing my Fuji Film; Thorlo for providing my socks; Leki for providing my trekking poles; Linda Doyle, Jenna Samelson, and Craig Keyzer at Westcliffe Publishers; the folks at the Egg Nest in Hachita; Bob Julyan; the Gendron family; Robert Lopez and the Silver City Fire Department; Mimbres Store; Tim Pohlman for the buckets of food and the route info in the Gila; Lester Jackson in Pie Town; Michele Ray and family in Grants for taking me in; Connie Dempsey for a place to get well when I was ill; Bitterweed Bob and Jim—long live mountain men; and all the people from the Land of Enchantment for their southern-style hospitality and smiles.

For Karyn.

—David Patterson

Author David Patterson checks his trail map in the Big Hatchet Mountains.

Opposite: *A yucca takes center stage while the Big Hatchet Mountains form the backdrop in the Bootheel region of southwestern New Mexico.*

11

PREFACE

The rain beat on my truck cab roof all night. I was stuck, really stuck, on my way to another Continental Divide trailhead. This time I had driven not only my four-wheel-drive vehicle into the mud, but my horse trailer with two llamas inside. How many times was this—four or five? I was hoping to be on my way, off to another carefree jaunt through forest and meadow. Instead, I knew the morning would bring a round of digging in the mud and helping the tow truck operator save my bacon.

Every part of New Mexico—north, south, mountain, plain, desert, and valley—at some point found me stuck in the mud during my search for photographs along the Continental Divide Trail. Getting to the trailheads in a series of El Niño years almost always proved the trickiest part of my journeys.

Also, should you decide to hike all or part of this trail throughout New Mexico, watch out for lightning. I barely survived some of the most horrific, yet spectacular, lightning storms imaginable while working on this project. During one, I counted three dozen strikes less than a mile from where I lay prostrate in a bed of hailstones, praying for my life.

Was all this worth the hassle and risk? Seeing a magnificent rainbow arc across the Aldo Leopold Wilderness, watching a rare fog dissipate in the Big Hatchet Mountains near the Mexican border, and admiring the giant fields of daisies and asters that carpet the plains around Pie Town are experiences that I will always carry with me. I walked in forests that, nurtured by the summer monsoons, were as verdant and lush as any in the nation; I struggled across black lava fields and parched badlands where claret cup cactus blooms dotted the landscape; I slept under golden aspen boughs on deserted mesas. It was a lot of fun.

I discovered a world along New Mexico's Continental Divide that doesn't typify the commonly held picture of southwestern tourism. Very few of the places depicted in this book, if any, are among the icons of Western scenery, yet their great diversity and beauty rival anything I've found elsewhere. Take for example the Sawtooth Mountains near Pie Town; very few people have heard of this small but enchanting range of pink granitic spires. The outlier ruins of Chaco Canyon near Grants were also a revelation to me. Though less imposing than Pueblo Bonito, these country cousins represent places where one can contemplate the mysteries of Ancestral Puebloan civilization in peace and quiet.

North of New Mexico, the Continental Divide Trail travels through a world of rock and tundra for most of its distance. But New Mexico's portion experiences a myriad of elevations, ecosystems, and landforms. Nowhere else on the trail can you encounter basin and range topography, true desert, dormant volcanoes and vast lava beds, sandstone canyons, and flattop mesas, all in one place. In addition to this topographic variety, the plant and animal life probably thrives more abundantly here than anywhere else along the Continental Divide Trail. Where else can you find a tarantula?

The area above the Rio Chama near Abiquiu bursts with vegetation in summer (opposite) and sleeps beneath a blanket of snow in winter (above).

Showy daisy carpets a field near Pie Town.

I found this route to harbor a great number of paradoxes. Though I had read about the supposed dislike of outsiders in some areas of New Mexico, but the friendliness of native New Mexicans and the kindness and respect with which I was treated amazed me. People in Catron County, for example, always waved as I passed them in my camper; no one seemed to care that a photographer was snooping around in the area. I always got a hearty wave while shooting near roads where passersby could see me work.

While photographing the Continental Divide Trail and spots along and near the Continental Divide, I tried to be sensitive to local people who oppose having the official path run near their communities. The photographs featured in this book represent the parts of the trail officially designated by the Continental Divide Trail Alliance, nearby scenic areas, and places along the actual Continental Divide where the trail will never go. For instance, I do not mean to imply by showing the true Continental Divide on the Jicarilla Apache Reservation or areas in the Carson National Forest that the official trail will ever go there. However, I do feel that allowing visitors to pass through an area on the Continental Divide Trail may carry with it fewer social problems, and probably pump as much money into the local economy, as the institution of gambling casinos.

Many of the Native American tribes who live on or near the Continental Divide in New Mexico consider the peaks along its length to be sacred land, and I imagine that anyone hiking the trail through these singular areas would feel the same. Pilgrims on their own quests through this country will discover the true Southwest, a land that has to be experienced on its own terms, and a land that exists completely apart from the frenetic world of twenty-first-century America.

— Tom Till
Moab, Utah

Opposite: *Atsinna Ruin in El Morro National Monument tells the tale of ancient Zuni culture.*

INTRODUCTION

History, I've heard, repeats itself. For me it's the repetition of footsteps, millions of them. Since 1995 my feet have carried me from Georgia to Maine and from Mexico to Canada twice. You could say I'm stricken with wanderlust, and an insatiable sense of adventure—perhaps the same things that drove Lewis and Clark to overcome insurmountable odds to explore the American West; but it's more than that. I love walking and living simply, and the trail provides the space to nourish my spirit like nowhere else in this world.

City life has never attracted me. I have spent a considerable part of my life leaving civilization behind, and in its wake I have discovered home. Out on the trail I am free, and the chains that bind us all are nonexistent. There aren't any demanding jobs, nagging bosses, ringing phones, beeping pagers, blaring televisions, speeding vehicles, or other such modern-day nuisances. It's a place where freedom reigns and wilderness abounds. The Continental Divide Trail (CDT), designated a National Scenic Trail in 1978, is one of these special places.

For the person seeking adventure, the Continental Divide corridor is probably one of the few existing wild stretches in the lower 48 states, and many portions of the CDT remain incomplete. Including countless miles of land managed by the Bureau of

The author greets the Colorado–New Mexico border.

Land Management (BLM), the CDT route in New Mexico passes through four National Forests, three Wilderness Areas, and one National Monument. The diverse terrain ranges from snow-capped peaks and wide-open mesas to sage-covered desert and sheer-walled canyons.

From Mexico to Canada, I hiked nearly 3,000 miles in five months along America's largest watershed, the Continental Divide. Along the way I encountered numerous bears (including an adult male grizzly less than 20 feet away), mountain lions, wind gusts strong enough to flatten me during a whiteout blizzard, lightning strikes too close for comfort, extreme heat, days without food, and days without water. But the sheer adventure and natural beauty I found along the way made enduring the fears and hardships worthwhile. Come walk with me and see for yourself.

—David Patterson
Redstone, Colorado

Opposite: Granite boulders congregate in the San Pedro Parks Wilderness.

Snow-laden juniper branches and the volcanic neck of Cabezon Peak rise above the Rio Puerco Valley.

La Ventana natural arch soars near El Malpais National Conservation Area.

THE BOOTHEEL AND THE MALPAIS HILLS

● *Mexican Border to Hachita: The Bootheel*

A vast desert sleeps in middle-of-nowhere New Mexico. This is the Bootheel region, so named from its shape on a state map. Nearby is the southern terminus of the nearly 3,000-mile Continental Divide Trail (CDT) route between Mexico and Canada. An endless sea of prickly pear, mesquite, ocotillo, cholla, and yucca defines the landscape before my eyes. Except for the rusty barbed wire fence that marks the border between Mexico and the United States, this land knows no boundaries, natural or artificial, as far as I can see.

The late April sun is waning as Pat Harris, a business owner in Hachita, New Mexico, leaves me and my partner, Karyn Jilk, along with two New Mexicans named Joseph Gendron and Bob Julyan, two miles from the border at dilapidated adobe structure. Glad to return to solid ground after a bone-jarring 4x4 ride, I don't mind Harris dropping us off short of the border, even though it means extra miles to walk. Suddenly my reservations about beginning the first day of our journey from Mexico to Canada with two strangers evaporate into the seemingly endless Chihuahuan Desert. For Joseph, an engineer from Silver City, and Bob, a writer from Albuquerque, this is another milestone on a crusade to establish an official route with the Bureau of Land Management (BLM) through the Bootheel region of southern New Mexico.

Leaving the border behind, we top off our water bottles at a windmill-fed stock tank. A lone cottonwood grows below the overflow from a 1,000-gallon tank. The tree's massive size is testimony to the wind's power to draw water

Taking a break at the Separ Road junction on the way to Silver City.

from the earth; it's a true giant in comparison to its neighboring cacti, and the only real shade for miles.

Only foolish humans and a few creatures acclimated to desert extremes venture out during the heat of the day, so we seek refuge under chaparral, or in this case near a water source under a tree. In this part of the country surface water, such as a creek or stream, is scarce. Therefore windmills, which pump underground water from aquifers to the surface, are the primary water sources.

The Big Hatchet Mountains tower above the desert floor to the northwest. Though the actual Continental Divide defines the Animas Mountains some 20 or more miles west of the Big Hatchets, private land prevents travel along that portion of the Divide. Unfortunately this diversion of foot traffic is a common theme for significant parts of the CDT in New Mexico, and until a permanent route is established with private landowners and government land agencies, sections of the route are subject to speculation and individual choices. Although previous hikers have utilized Highway 81, which cuts through the barren Playas Valley from Antelope Wells Port of Entry to commence their journeys, we set off from the Mexican border just south of the craggy Big Hatchet Mountains to avoid walking a paved desert highway.

At 8,363 feet, Big Hatchet Peak disrupts the empty horizon. It's the first climb and the first mountain on the journey to Canada. The air is crisp and a breeze whips up dirt devils, tornado-like funnels of dust, in the barren flats behind us. Daylight is fading fast, but we continue hiking in search of a

Opposite: *Sunrise blurs the distinction between water and sky on the Gray Ranch Nature Conservancy Preserve in New Mexico's Bootheel.*

Mexican gold poppies spring from the soil of the Florida Mountains Wilderness Study Area.

"Except for the rusty barbed wire fence that marks the border between Mexico and the United States, this land knows no boundaries, natural or artificial, as far as I can see."

THE MAKING OF THE BOOTHEEL

Included in the 1848 Treaty of Guadalupe Hidalgo, which ended the Mexican-American War, was a map by a surveyor named John Disturnell. This map placed El Paso, Texas, 100 miles east and 34 miles north of where it is today. In order to resolve the dispute, the United States paid Mexico $10 million for the Gadsden Purchase of 1853. This transaction acquired for the United States the land south of the confluence of the Gila River and the Colorado River in Arizona all the way to the Rio Grande near El Paso. The dip in New Mexico's border, which defines the Bootheel, was to ensure that the United States would have a southern transcontinental railroad route across the Continental Divide and the Peloncillo Mountains. Accordingly, it was easier to draw straight lines on maps than to conduct surveys around geographic features like the Big and Little Hatchet mountains.

Wide-open grasslands blanket the Animas Valley near Cloverdale in New Mexico's Bootheel while the Animas Mountains rise in the background.

A barn crumbles in the ghost town of Cloverdale.

windmill where we hope to find water and a place to camp. After traveling several miles in an arroyo, a seasonal streambed, I climb its flanks and discover a lone windmill about 100 yards away, its blades churning from a steady evening breeze. A barbed wire fence divides two grazing allotments, and remnant dung piles mark the presence of roving cattle. The heavens outshine the earth as we scratch out a camp on the rocky ground beneath a midnight sky and an ocean of stars.

From the windmill the primitive jeep road disintegrates and we continue cross-country. It's almost as if the desert plants, not yet in full bloom, are begrudging of Karyn's bright and shiny new equipment. Every hundred yards or so one of them swipes something dangling from her pack. First it's her floral-print hat, then a compass with a cardinal red lanyard, and finally her canary yellow T-shirt soaked through with yesterday's perspiration. She has no idea and I cheerfully retrieve them for her as if I'm browsing through a desert bazaar.

Within an hour the ascent is over and a steep scramble descent ensues. I see what appear to be caves off in the distance, perhaps cliff dwellings. Joseph breaks away from us to investigate a proposed BLM route, so we take time to explore the cliffs. There are signs of life, a previous existence: the rock

Morning fog enshrouds the Big Hatchet Mountains after a heavy rain.

ceilings and walls are blackened by fire; miniature corn cobs and pestle holes in the rock indicate food was ground, prepared, and eaten here. Bob finds an arrowhead on the trail, and ultimately decides to leave it. It's amazing how the tools, clothing, and weapons of these previous cultures are merely modifications of the natural environment: rock, wood, and bone. They blend in, unlike our plastics and synthetic materials, eventually returning back to the earth with time.

We're not even 50 miles from the border and I can see several fast-moving vehicles racing south on Highway 81. I've never known anyone that eager to get anywhere. Traveling at top speed, one truck nearly wrecks while braking after spotting us. It's the border patrol and they've been looking for us, or rather the owners of the suspicious footprints, near the border. Without any formal greeting they ask to see our shoe treads and promptly radio to headquarters, "We found them!" Well, we aren't missing and we certainly aren't illegal aliens so they let us go, all the while shaking their heads at why anybody would voluntarily hike through this country. I admit it's a bit unusual, but it's part of the whole. Besides, in life, as well as on the trail, you have to accept the good with the bad—or you won't make it.

Next page: Mexican gold poppies unfurl in the morning sunlight in the Florida Mountains Wilderness Study Area near Deming.

The Mimbres culture created this petroglyph, located south of Cookes Peak in Luna County.

⬭ *Hachita to Silver City: The Malpais Hills*

The third day out Karyn and I arrive in Hachita, a dwindling town 50 miles from the Mexican border. Bob and Joseph have gone, but I am thankful for their companionship and route information. Like the cliff dwellings behind us, there are meager signs of life in Hachita. Worn-out tires adorn the roofs of dilapidated trailers (later I learn that the tires prevent the metal roofs from rattling or working their way loose in the wind), and junk cars are strewn across many of the yards in town. Perhaps Hachita was once prosperous, as the immense cemetery on the outskirts of town indicates, but not now. Today there are merely a couple

> *"It's amazing how the tools, clothing, and weapons of these previous cultures are merely modifications of the natural environment: rock, wood, and bone."*

of places to buy gas and snacks, a rodeo arena, numerous weathered buildings, and, surprisingly, a post office. Nevertheless what defines this place are the people who eke out a modest existence in the seemingly inhospitable desert: they stop for you, even if they're late for work, to see if you need a ride, water, or help. It's ironic, but typically the people who have the least offer you the most. I am thankful for the hearty souls who reside here.

From Hachita the route is obscure at best. Ultimately we opt to follow the rolling crests of the Cedar Mountain Range toward Interstate 10. Though we've only been out a few days, we're steadily falling into a daily routine: wake up early to escape the unrelenting sun, drink as much water as possible, find more water, find shade during the heat of the day, eat, sleep, and repeat the same process over and over. In camp

Outcrops of volcanic rock blaze at sunset in the Malpais Hills.

Clouds graze the lofty Cookes Peak, as seen from near City of Rocks State Park.

"It's ironic, but typically the people who have the least offer you the most. I am thankful for the hearty souls who reside here."

RANCHING IN THE DESERT

A desert "oasis"—an underground water system along the Piedra Lumbre.

Amazingly enough, cattle graze in the desert—hence the windmills, which provide water to thirsty bovines and other desert flora and fauna. Ranches are typically composed of 640-acre sections of land. Because desert vegetation, including grama grass, is sparse, one section barely supports eight to 15 head of cattle. It boggles the mind that cattle, let alone humans, can survive these desert extremes.

Mexican gold poppies accent the Continental Divide Trail at Separ.

Karyn sets up our tent and I cook our home-dehydrated meals of eggplant Parmesan, various pastas with sauce, and an assortment of bean and rice dishes. Some might think that an odd arrangement, but in truth Karyn is a pyromaniac. It's a short story—all for the sake of cooking some pasta, she nearly torched the entire Anza-Borrego Desert in Southern California when hiking the Pacific Crest Trail. So we figure it's best that I cook until we get into some wetter climes.

Contrary to popular belief, this journey isn't a leisurely jaunt in the woods, or desert, for that matter. There's plenty of time for hiking, though little else. I write in my journal at night and sometimes read if I'm restless. Otherwise, life is reduced down to its simplest terms: food, water, and shelter.

Nearing Bessie Rhoads Mountain I call in at the Thorn Ranch for water. Numerous cattle dogs announce my arrival. At the main ranch house I learn nobody speaks English. It's a Mexican-owned and operated ranch. Fortunately my Spanish isn't too rusty and Oscar, the ranch manager, informs me of the *molinos de vientos* (windmills) ahead. We are low on food and itchy to reach Silver City. It is a couple days' walk from here, so we hike on into the night after politely declining his generous offer to stay.

Closing in on the Malpais Hills we meet Matt McDonald, the youngest son of the family-owned and operated McDonald Ranch, out plying the backroads in a well-worn pickup truck. He informs us where we can find water along the Separ Road to White Signal, and I can't help but notice the fiery, faraway look in his eyes—the look of someone who spends all his days in the desert. As Matt promised, the water holes are dispersed at frequent intervals, no more than 10 miles apart, which is excellent for this semi-barren landscape.

The Tyrone Mine and other private lands obstruct the route to Silver City. Therefore we reluctantly follow Highway 90 into town. It is the first paved route for us in New Mexico and it's somewhat dreadful. Our goal is to avoid paved roads because they are dangerous and motorists unpredictable. Also, they're generally not as scenic or interesting as hiking cross-country or on a trail, and injuries such as tendonitis are prevalent from the repetitive pounding one must endure while plodding along a

"Contrary to popular belief, this journey isn't a leisurely jaunt in the woods, or desert, for that matter."

road. Though the route is less than 15 miles, it's enough to wreak havoc on Karyn's feet. In Silver City we gratefully accept the hospitality of Robert Lopez and the crew of the Silver City Fire Department. Karyn's feet look like raw meat after a week on the trail, and we are thankful for the fire department's offer to rest and heal before heading into the 3.3-million acre Gila National Forest.

The Big Burro Mountains near Silver City loom in the distance across an open field.

GILA NATIONAL FOREST

Silver City to Pie Town: Gila National Forest

On May 6, we depart Silver City and enter the Gila National Forest. Old mining camps litter the landscape, and pines dominate the forest. Agave, prickly pear, and other high-desert plants creep into its environs. There's shade enough, at least what the pines and junipers offer. On the summits, trees are snapped in half and pines ooze sap from their scars—including CDT markers nailed into trees. There is actual trail in part of the Gila, though it still feels remote and wild.

Nearing the first surface water for miles, I encounter a mountain man named Jim. His camp is a stone's throw away, and he informs me it's an old mining claim. Jim is an old-timer and his appearance harkens back to that of a miner from an age long gone. His voice is raspy from too many unfiltered cigarettes, and the glare in his eyes reveals he's far more comfortable in the woods than anywhere else in society. I know how he feels. Surprisingly, Jim invites us to stay for a while and breaks out fruit punch and moonshine while Karyn and I offer up cheese sandwiches and lemonade.

Karyn befriends Jim's puppy, Sioux. Jim inquires about our hike while they play. I inform him that we intend to hike from Mexico to Canada along the Continental Divide. His reaction takes me by surprise: he wants to know if I'm "prospectin'" along the way. Obviously I say the wrong thing because Jim disappears behind his rig in a wave of disgust. A few minutes later he comes back with a gold pan accompanied by a gargantuan spoon and throws them at my feet. "Here, you need this mor'n I do."

The author negotiates snags in the Gila Wilderness near Diamond Peak.

Though I appreciate his offer, I just spent the better part of a day paring down my gear for this stretch, which is probably the greatest distance between towns along the entire CDT. Nevertheless, Jim is persistent and it takes me a while to convince him I can't afford to prospect along the way. After all, I'm searching for a different kind of gold.

The Gila is a refuge from the surrounding desert, a solitary fortress. Notwithstanding, the going is tough and the trails are steep—probably why not many people hike here. Water is scarce, too, owing to the fact that it's a relatively dry year. Climbing into the Black Range, part of the Aldo Leopold Wilderness, I find water in a cistern adjacent to Reeds Peak Fire Tower and Cabin. It seems like the only reliable water sources are either windmills or developed springs, and sometimes they're not even reliable. The views are astounding from the lofty heights of the fire tower, and the cabin is a welcome refuge from the biting cold above 10,000 feet, so we decide to spend the night here.

The north-facing slopes still retain a fair amount of snow, which impedes our progress. Topping out on a ridge, we enter a forest recovering from a massive fire. Lush green stalks adorn the hillsides. A herd of elk, including three enormously racked bulls, moves forth and retreats as gracefully as snowflakes descending upon the earth. Unfortunately the route is a messy jumble of trees, and the trail we are searching for has eroded in the years since the fire.

Bushwhacking isn't necessarily my favorite pastime, but it's what we have to do to get beyond Diamond Peak. It's almost as if a bulldozer piled all

Opposite: Yuccas punctuate a golden desert grassland below Bear Mountain in Gila National Forest.

Leaves pile up along the Continental Divide Trail in the Black Range.

these trees on top of each other, but then again Mother Nature's power is awesome. When the wind howls the few standing dead snags sway, and I can hear their eerie voices shrieking from the flames that licked them not long ago. Because this is a Wilderness Area, and power tools such as chain saws are not permitted, it will take years for crosscut saws to cut a path through these blowdowns. By chance, I find a path that's not even on the map; it leads us through Doubtful Canyon and on toward the Beaverhead Work Station.

Nearly out of food from the additional days spent trying to find a way through the blowdowns and well over 100 miles from the next town, we encounter Tim Pohlman, a ranger, just as he's returning from

> *"When the wind howls the few standing dead snags sway, and I can hear their eerie voices . . ."*

feeding a crew fighting a fire on the other side of the forest. In the back of his monstrous, dually diesel crew cab truck are numerous five-gallon buckets of eggs, biscuits, potatoes, and orange juice—a starving hiker's dream come true. He promptly invites us back to his cabin and we readily devour the leftovers. After an hour of conversation, Tim instructs us to take all we can because it will just go to waste. Without hesitation I fill all of our empty zip-lock bags to the brim, thankful for his generosity and kindness.

We leave the Gila and its magical canyons and forests behind as we head toward Pie Town. In the desert again, I feel like a modern-day Don Quixote searching for a windmill, except my intention isn't combat, but refreshment from its life-bearing water. We arrive at a windmill marked on the map, but it's completely devoid of water. Its mechanisms are in

An agave clings to a rock outcrop in the Gila National Forest.

A cave dwelling hides in a cliff face at Gila Cliff Dwellings National Monument.

ruins and the tank is dry. This is getting serious. We need to find water, a precious commodity in the middle of nowhere. A couple of hours and eight miles later, I discover another windmill. Though there's water and we are beyond thirsty, a decomposing vulture floats on its murky surface. No chance I'm drinking that, even though I've been forced to drink worse in the past. Don't ask. We press on, our mouths thick as cotton and brimming with sand grit, our heads pounding from dehydration. Steps ahead of the approaching dusk, we encounter another windmill. Thankfully, water flows from its spout. The cool water soothes our sunburned lips and parched throats. We make camp, drinking more than we eat for dinner.

Back on public lands managed by the BLM—and nonetheless wary, as it signifies no relief from the lack of water—we cross the Divide near Coyote Peak. The Plains of San Agustin, where we are heading, stretch out to the north. It looks barren; it is barren. As I traverse the shadeless plains, the sun scorches the backsides of my legs. Thousands of grasshoppers take flight in the prevailing spring winds and pound us like winged pellets of

A thunderhead builds at sunset, as viewed from Hillsboro Peak in the Aldo Leopold Wilderness.

hail. We have been out for nearly two weeks since Silver City, and once again our food is nearly gone. The ferocious wind seems to push me back a few paces every time I step forward. It feels like we aren't getting any closer to Pie Town and its fabled post office, where our food parcel awaits.

The desiccated ground beneath our feet is cracked like a jigsaw puzzle. Tramping across the latticework of dry mud feels like walking on crusty snow—we sink a few inches with every step. I stick the tip of my hiking pole into a partially evaporated mud hole; the spoiled stench of sulphur emanates from the opening. The going is slow and we end up camping near a windmill in the exposed chaparral of the Plains of San Agustin.

Though it's the middle of May, I awake to discover my water bottle frozen. I can hardly believe it, but looking back I see fresh snow on the Gila's peaks glistening in the sun. At Old Horse Springs the gravity of our situation weighs upon me like a lead zeppelin. It's Friday afternoon and we're still about 30 miles from Pie Town. The post office closes early on Saturday, and there is nowhere in town to purchase groceries. We have to make it to

Sunflowers populate the ghost town of Chloride.

"Tramping across the latticework of dry mud feels like walking on crusty snow—we sink a few inches with every step."

the post office, our only food source, but we are weak from hiking big miles while rationing our food. Karyn laments that all she has left is an instant split-pea concoction. She cringes at the thought of eating it despite the fact that she's starving. Out of love I swap her my remaining food, a 500-calorie bear claw, for her meager instant split peas. I choke down the peas and she ravages my bear claw, simultaneously expressing her gratitude and dismay.

A lone Ponderosa pine greets the sunrise on Burnt Cabin Flat in the Gila National Forest.

Next page: *A glorious winter sunrise burns the sky over the Plains of San Agustin.*

Rock outcrops pepper the O-Bar-O Mesa area on the south side of Pelona Mountain.

GILA NATIONAL FOREST

Once a stronghold for Apache warrior Geronimo and his followers, the Gila National Forest boasts 3.3 million acres of publicly owned forest, canyons, and desert. Within the Gila National Forest lies the Gila Wilderness. In June 1924, the Gila Wilderness was designated as the world's first wilderness. Forty years later, the U.S. Forest Service defined such wilderness as "an area where the earth and its community of life are untrammeled by man, where man himself is a visitor who does not remain."

The Continental Divide meanders for nearly 200 miles through this spectacular country. The elevation ranges from 4,200 feet to almost 11,000 feet, and four of the six life zones are represented. Deer, elk, antelope, and bighorn sheep abound, as well as wild turkeys, black bears, and mountain lions.

The rust-colored cliffs of the Sawtooth Range bask in the sunlight.

Next page: *A summer storm settles in over the broad rangeland of Catron County.*

THE HIGH-DESERT COUNTRY AND MT. TAYLOR

Pie Town to Grants: High-Desert Country

Early the next morning we make it to the post office in Pie Town before it closes. Thankfully our parcel is there, but we've already grown weary of the rice and beans, pastas, and energy bars we packaged months ago. It's not that the food tastes bad—in fact it's quite good—but this is my third thru-hike in four years and my vegetarian diet hasn't varied much in that time. Being a vegetarian is difficult on the trail, especially when we visit ranching communities like Pie Town. This area, like most of the Divide corridor, is beef country, where the only restaurant in town seems to serve nothing but steak or some variation thereof, morning, noon, and night. Nevertheless, most small-town restaurants are accommodating and we order what we can for variety.

Pie Town's name derives from the fact that long ago, someone used to bake and sell pies here. A local tells me it's the former pinto bean capital of the United States, which explains the array of rusty machinery and tractors lying about. The 1940s saw much more precipitation here, but now, because of a marked decrease in rain, ranching has replaced farming. Today most folks in these parts earn their living from cattle ranching.

Pie Town resident Lester Jackson, a war veteran, greets us with a warm welcome. We camp at the only facility in town, Jackson Camp and Park. By the entrance a sign announces free camping, the name "Lester" conspicuously inserted above "Jackson." Lester informs us that he added his first name so nobody would come along later and fill in "Jesse" or some other name. In 1980 the BLM turned the 75-acre parcel over to Lester and

Karyn Jilk hikes in Zuni Canyon west of Grants.

the town. Lester has been adding to the park and camp for everyone's enjoyment ever since.

Rabbits, antelope herds, and sagebrush abound. This is high desert, nearly 8,000 feet. It's also home to the alligator juniper, its fire-ravaged bark resembling an alligator's hide. We pass the old Lehue Store north of Pie Town. Two brothers operated a business here until a fight ensued, and one of them built another shop two miles down the road. Though it appears this dusty miles-from-nowhere road once served as a major thoroughfare, the buildings, one of stone and the other of log, are now in a state of ruin.

Ahead, the El Malpais National Monument (*el malpais* is Spanish for "the badlands") breaks the continuity of the scenery. It's one of the best examples of "recently" formed volcanic landscapes in the country, and its immense lava flow forms a natural boundary, directing travel around it. Sticking to the west side of the flow, we follow game trails that lead us to water.

The hardened rock is impressive, a jumble of intricately woven shards and blocks of lava. It's obvious why few people attempt to travel through it, though an ancient trade route, the Zuni-Acoma Trail, proves otherwise. Regardless, we decide to stay near the Divide and arrive at Oso Ridge, where a lookout tower juts up from a pinnacle summit. For the first time I can clearly see Mount Taylor. In the eastern horizon, it rises high above the desert floor to an elevation of 11,301 feet. El Malpais National Monument expands to the south, and to the north lie the canyonlands of the Navajo Nation. The views are absolutely astounding.

Opposite: *Slender pinnacles pierce the sky in Cibola National Forest.*

We soon enter the Cibola National Forest, the first National Forest since the Gila in southern New Mexico. The pine and aspen trees provide shade, a welcome change from the desert, and the snow on Mount Taylor assures me there's water ahead. From here the Continental Divide defines the Zuni Mountains as the range arcs west and north. The CDT route takes advantage of the area's public lands, continuing through the Cibola National Forest toward the highway town of Grants.

THE CIBOLA NATIONAL FOREST AND MOUNT TAYLOR

The Cibola National Forest includes two separate mountain ranges: the Zuni Mountains west of Grants and the San Mateo Mountains northeast of Grants. The most prominent feature of the San Mateo Mountains is the extinct volcano, Mount Taylor. Once known as Mount San Mateo, it was renamed Mount Taylor in 1849 for then president Zachary Taylor by a lieutenant on a military expedition against the Navajos. The lieutenant probably knew the local Spanish name, but likely assumed it should have an American name because New Mexico had recently been annexed. Besides San Mateo, Hispanics also have called it Cebolleta, meaning "little onion," as well as names in at least nine American Indian languages. It rises to an elevation of 11,301 feet, and a spruce-fir forest thrives near the summit.

Rainwater pools in the lava flows of El Malpais National Monument near Mount Taylor.

An azure New Mexico sky is framed from within a lava tube at El Malpais National Monument.

Next page: The lava flows and sandstone cliffs of El Malpais National Monument expand beneath the sunset, as viewed from Sandstone Bluffs Overlook.

Big paintbrush brightens the landscape near the town of Cuba.

◉ *Grants to Cuba: Mount Taylor*

In Grants we meet Michele Ray, a postal employee, who offers to take us in for the night. The wonderful people of New Mexico somehow always find us whenever we're in need of a place to rest and wash off the grime from the trail. This isn't the first time we've accepted the hospitality of someone new; it seems like nobody in rural New Mexico is a stranger. It's the goodwill of others I meet that renews my spirit and faith in Americans. I think this is what it must have been like for my grandfather when he, also struck by wanderlust, set out across the country. I am thankful there are places that still exist where people aren't afraid to help somebody.

Mount Taylor beckons and we leave Grants behind via Lobo Canyon Road, the most direct route back into the Cibola National Forest. Along the way we pass the state penitentiary. The razor-sharp barbed wire fence creeps right up to the road, and several inmates are out in the yard. Sometimes I feel trapped on a long hike, especially when the weather is miserable, but then again I make the daily choice to be here and realize the power in my decision is freedom. One guy ambles up close to the fence and calls out to us, "Hey, where you goin'?" For a minute I think he might try to harass us, but he is genuinely interested and even more perplexed when I tell him we're walking to Canada. As we pass by he shouts, "We'll see you on the way back, then."

Mount Taylor, once known as Mount San Mateo, is the biggest mountain around for miles. More than just a landmark, the mountain holds serious religious significance for several American Indian tribes including the Acoma, Laguna, Navajo, and Zuni. Noting this, the Forest Service has yet to reach an agreement on the designated route up and over the holy mountain. Apparently certain sacred sites exist on and adjacent to Mount Taylor, but the way I see it, every mountain is sacred. It disturbs me that roads cut almost all the way to the summit—

Colorful yellow lichen covers the lava in El Malpais National Monument.

The Chaco culture's Casamero Ruins glow in the September sunlight.

another defilement by humans—and cattle graze well above 10,000 feet on its grassy flanks.

This is probably the biggest climb in New Mexico save for a few steep ups and downs in the Gila. On top, I look back to visualize our route, but the smoky haze in the sky from fires raging in Mexico obscures my view.

The north-facing slopes are laden with snow. Nevertheless we traverse them without too much difficulty. Fields of fresh green grass and wildflowers cover the lower mountainside, and water and elk abound. In the distance I see the all-encompassing desert and realize we will soon leave the fruits of this beautiful mountain behind. Before I leave this island in the desert—a veritable oasis—I enjoy a frigid dip in a snowmelt-fed stream. The water is freezing, yet refreshing. It does wonders for my swollen feet. I feel a sense of rebirth and revel in the birdsong from the surrounding forest as I drip dry.

A POWERFUL THIRST

The sun is relentless in the desert. There are days when I simply long for a cloud—a cloud that will follow me all day like an umbrella. My mouth stays dry no matter how much I drink. One day I consume nearly 20 liters (about 5 gallons) of water. More often than not, livestock contaminates the water here. Nevertheless it's the only water for miles and I have to drink it to survive, even if it means getting sick from the microorganisms that thrive in the polluted water. For these occasions I take a prescription—whatever makes my stomach churn will soon abate after a few pills and a couple days of rest.

La Ventana Arch, the state's second largest natural span, stretches across the sky in El Malpais National Conservation Area.

Mount Taylor crowns the bluffs at Sandstone Bluffs Overlook in El Malpais National Monument.

Sunset colors showcase Cabezon Peak, an ancient volcanic plug, along the Continental Divide Trail.

A claret cup cactus blooms on the forest floor in El Malpais National Monument.

"There are days when I simply long for a cloud—a cloud that will follow me all day like an umbrella."

Back on BLM land, the water sources are few and far between. Earth stock tanks, actually miniature man-made ponds, offer water, however it's supersaturated with dirt, and cattle and elk frequently wallow in the tanks. We take our chances on the few unreliable springs in the desert because the sediment and other contaminants in the earth stock tanks will clog any water filter in just a few pumps. Even pre-filtering the water with a bandanna doesn't help; after passing through the tightly woven cloth, the liquid is just as brown as it was before. Therefore we generally have to carry water upwards of 20 miles until we find another water source. Entering the Ignacio Chavez Land Grant, a Wilderness Study Area, I find a small oasis in the form of a trickling cold-water spring known as Ojo de los Indios. Beyond the Ignacio Chavez the landscape changes. The route descends into open mesas with rolling hills, sheer cliffs, and rocky outcrops. The contrast is amazing, though water sources are increasingly infrequent along the route to Cuba.

Perched above the lava flows, sandstone pools collect rainwater in El Malpais National Monument near Mount Taylor.

Next page: *Cabezon Peak and a nearby mesa anchor the landscape in the Rio Puerco area.*

Cuba to Ghost Ranch: San Pedro Parks Wilderness

Cuba isn't much of a town, but Flora Ward, proprietor of the Cuban Lodge, rushes out to greet us. In her office she presents photographs of previous Continental Divide hikers. Her enthusiasm for the trail and its hikers is infectious, but as it stands, I'm infected with something else and I find it difficult to withstand the desire to hurl. Fortunately, our friend from the beginning of the trip, Bob Julyan, has a relative in the area, Connie Dempsey, who invites us to recuperate at her ranch in Upper La Jara.

After four wonderful days off, we enter the San Pedro Parks Wilderness, part of the Santa Fe National Forest, where dandelion, Indian paintbrush, lupine, and iris bloom with wild abandon. After the initial climb, the terrain mellows and opens into the expansive meadows that define the San Pedro Parks. Pockets of spruce and fir tower in clusters along with the occasional aspen grove. Rapidly melting snow makes the parks rather swampy. Still we traverse the residual snowdrifts with ease, owing to the parks' tabletop topography. Signs of beaver mark all the waterways, and elk rejoice in spring's succulent green grasses.

By luck or coincidence, we run into Allan Stibora, an Albuquerque resident and CDT advocate, just north of the San Pedro Parks. He's scouting a route for the Continental Divide Trail Society (CDTS) and informs us of the CDTS's proposed route through the Carson National Forest. Noting that we're at a crossroads, and considering our natural tendency to avoid paved routes, we decide to go for it without hesitation, even though it means extra miles and several more days before we reach Colorado.

The route descends into the Chama River Canyon Wilderness. Actual tread, a thin ribbon of marked trail, courses its way to the river. Reminiscent of the trail in the San Pedro Parks, it's a nice change from constantly bushwhacking. From the Rio Chama we follow a fenceline and a dirt road to the famous grounds of Ghost Ranch.

Author David Patterson hikes across a snowfield.

Karyn's been raving about Ghost Ranch ever since she read about it in *Where the Waters Divide: A Walk Along America's Continental Divide*, a book by Karen Berger and Daniel Smith. Run by the Presbyterian church, Ghost Ranch is a sprawling spiritual retreat center. With more than 21,000 acres, the ranch includes a nationally known conference center, three museums, a 24-hour library, and the former summer home and studio of artist Georgia O'Keeffe.

We follow a nature trail across a swinging bridge to the conference center, where we find even more than we bargained for—an all-you-can-eat, buffet-style dinner in the cafeteria. After burning thousands of calories a day on the trail, that's something no long-distance hiker can pass up. Along with sumo wrestlers, long-distance hikers are among the few visitors to all-you-can-eat buffets who actually get told, "That's all you can eat!" So after my fifth pass through the line, I'm grateful to the grandmotherly woman who offers me vegetable lasagna and a smile every time.

Opposite: *Rime ice coats aspen trees in Carson National Forest.*

● *Ghost Ranch to Colorado Border: Tierra Amarilla*

Beyond the towering red mesa cliffs surrounding Ghost Ranch Conference Center lies a box canyon, and above sits the Carson National Forest. A faint path diverges from the well-worn box canyon trail, climbing a steep and rocky route into Carson National Forest. Few trails exist within this portion of the National Forest, and when I call on a U.S. Forest Service ranger for route information, he informs me he wants it to remain that way. So do the descendants of the original inhabitants of the area designated by the Tierra Amarilla Land Grant. For years, Carson National Forest has supported their livelihoods by providing timber and lush rangeland. Unfortunately, the locals are threatened by the prospect of the Continental Divide Trail passing through their extended backyard. They believe the trail will jeopardize their traditional way of life and use of the forest. Regardless, at this time it's public land and the going is easy, with or without the trail.

A row of evergreens borders a meadow in the San Pedro Parks Wilderness.

Traveling cross-country, we accidentally stumble onto private land. I realize we might be in over our heads when a fantastic log cabin comes into view and a pack of dogs alerts the owner of our presence. My first instinct is to turn back, but when I see a man with a pistol on his hip and a rifle in his hand, I know he's looking for whatever is causing his dogs to bark. Rather than surprise a man bearing arms, I call out a friendly "Hello!"—the kind of hello that's meant to say, "I know I'm not supposed to be here, so please don't shoot." After an exchange of names, Bitterweed Bob invites us back to his cabin. He's friendly, and after another hard winter spent alone above 10,000 feet, he's eager to welcome us into his home. Bob tells us he's the only person to winter up here. Though there are a few other homes across the mountainside, he truly has no neighbors and uses a snowmobile to get home in the winter, which at this elevation can last more than seven months out of the year. Like Prospector Jim down in the Gila, Bitterweed Bob is a modern-day mountain

Cabezon Peak (left) and Cerro Cochino (right) overlook the Ancestral Puebloan Guadalupe Pueblo Ruin.

Next page: The *cliffs of Red Mesa and Sierra Nacimiento color the southern Jemez Mountains.*

The Nogales Cliff House is cached within Santa Fe National Forest.

man living in an age-old tradition. Bob relates with hard-won pride how he built his log cabin from trees he cut and milled on his land. From his expertly constructed cabin to his hand-carved walking sticks, he's definitely a craftsman. He impresses Karyn and me because he lives off the grid, without electricity from a power company. His system entails a few solar panels and deep-cycle batteries. He heats his house by burning wood, mainly using trees blown down during the winter. From his renewable energy to his spring-fed water system, Bob is self-sufficient—much better off than most people these days.

Nearing the Colorado–New Mexico border, we continue cross-country through Carson National Forest and part of the Tierra Amarilla. The spectacular lushness of the terrain—the rivers, forests, and grass-lands—nurtures our senses after all the harsh miles logged in the desert.

HISPANIC SHEPHERDS

Throughout the forests of northern New Mexico, Hispanic shepherds have carved their cultural niche into the soft, white bark of aspen trees, their designs becoming more readable as the tree grows. Carvings of female nudes, either lewd or artistic, are among the most common, but some carvings relay information about troublesome bears or coyotes, the location of a spring, or directions to a neighboring shepherd's camp. These carvings exemplify the shepherds' solitary existence in the mountains. According to experts, the most detailed carvings are the ones scratched out with a slight incision rather than a deep gouge. Apparently carving does not affect the health of the tree, but it is not encouraged today.

Morning casts its clear light on the Rio Chama in the Chama River Canyon Wilderness.

The sculpted form of Chimney Rock overlooks Ghost Ranch.

Rather than rush into Colorado, we decide to savor one more night in New Mexico, even though we're merely a stone's throw from the border. We camp about 150 yards off a Forest Service road within a grove of spruce trees. Though I hesitate to camp near a road, even if it's a seldom-used Forest Service road, Karyn thinks we'll be okay hidden in the trees. In contrast with our leisurely pace, the second storm of the trip passes by in a hurry to get to Colorado. Though it rains hard for an hour, the intricately woven spruce limbs overhead keep us dry.

"It's hard to imagine we've come this far, nearly 800 miles on foot."

We give thanks daily for the simple things: water, food, shelter, and each other. It's hard to imagine we've come this far, nearly 800 miles on foot. But dwelling within my memories of the miles behind us, my reflections on New Mexico are as clear as the sun's rays parting the turbulent flow of a cascading waterfall in the Gila Wilderness. I've joyously reveled in places that haven't felt the heavy footsteps of humankind—magical places where the sands of time are measured by the articulate hands and coursing breath of nature. I've tasted sweet, pure spring water filtered by the earth; hidden from the unrelenting sun beneath the welcome shade of piñon and juniper trees too many times to remember; and chased down rainbows that arc across bright, steel-blue skies. Along with this state's colorful cast of characters—weathered ranchers, forest rangers, mountain men, and friendly strangers—it's nature's own character, silently revealing herself to me in the canyons, deserts, and mountains of New Mexico, that has made my journey through the Land of Enchantment an everlasting experience.

A wall of ice shimmers in Box Canyon at Ghost Ranch near the Rio Chama.

Next page: *The southern tip of Mesa Golondrina hovers above the confluence of Rio Chama and Rio Gallina.*

A wall of sandstone distinguishes Echo Amphitheater, near the Rio Chama.

TIERRA AMARILLA

Tierra Amarilla (Spanish for "yellow earth" or "yellow land") is a Spanish-American village located in northern New Mexico. Originally named Las Nutrias for the many beaver that made their home in the area, the village was later named Tierra Amarilla to reflect the abundance of yellow clay deposits found in the area.

Though part of an 1832 Mexican land grant, Tierra Amarilla was not permanently settled by Hispanics until 1862 for fear of raids by Utes, Jicarilla Apaches, and Navajos.

Spanish is the universal language of this mountain community, though, as in many early New Mexican colonies, lack of daily contact with Mexico during the seventeenth, eighteenth, and nineteenth centuries hindered the modernization of language here. The speech of Tierra Amarilla's denizens is fraught with sixteenth- and seventeenth-century forms now obsolete in other Spanish-speaking parts of the world. Through the years, New Mexican settlers like those in Tierra Amarilla also adopted words and expressions from Mexican Indians, Rio Grande Indians, Mexican Spanish, and American English, thus creating a dialect unique to these isolated communities of New Mexico.

Cane cholla and sandstone cliffs commingle in Carson National Forest near Ghost Ranch.

Autumn gold colors the aspens on Mangas Mountain in Cibola National Forest.

The Almighty Aspen

The quaking aspen, a member of the willow family (*Salicaceae*), is closely related to various poplars such as the cottonwood. The most widely distributed tree in North America, it can be found from the mountains of Mexico to northern Alaska, from the Atlantic to the Pacific, from sea level to nearly 12,000 feet.

What's unusual about the quaking aspen is its ability to reproduce by a process called suckering. Individual stems sprout lateral roots that send up other erect stems. At a glance, these stems (called ramets) appear to be individual trees, but really form asingle genetic individual known as a clone. Aspen stands are known to be some of the world's largest living organisms.

Autumn oaks show their seasonal beauty on the Jicarilla Apache Reservation along the Continental Divide.

The still waters of Abiquiu Lake mirror the landscape downstream from Chama River Canyon Wilderness.

Wildflowers thrive in an open meadow in the Tusas Mountains east of Tierra Amarilla.

APPENDIX A
Bibliography and Suggested Reading

Berger, Karen, and Daniel R. Smith. *Where the Waters Divide: A Walk Along America's Continental Divide*. New York: Harmony Books, 1993.

Cobos, Ruben. *A Dictionary of New Mexico and Southern Colorado Spanish*. Santa Fe, N.M.: Museum of New Mexico Press, 1982.

Davis, Lora. *Wyoming's Continental Divide Trail: The Official Guide*. Englewood, Colo.: Westcliffe Publishers, 2000.

Fayhee, M. John. *Along Colorado's Continental Divide Trail*. Englewood, Colo.: Westcliffe Publishers, 1997.

Fugate, Francis L., and Roberta B. Fugate. *Roadside History of New Mexico*. Missoula, Mont.: Mountain Press Publishing Company, 1989.

Howard, Lynna. *Along Montana and Idaho's Continental Divide Trail*. Englewood, Colo.: Westcliffe Publishers, 2000.

_____. *Montana and Idaho's Continental Divide Trail: The Official Guide*. Englewood, Colo.: Westcliffe Publishers, 2000.

Jones, Tom Lorang. *Colorado's Continental Divide Trail: The Official Guide*. Englewood, Colo.: Westcliffe Publishers, 1997.

Julyan, Bob. *New Mexico's Continental Divide Trail: The Official Guide*. Englewood, Colo.: Westcliffe Publishers, 2001.

_____. *The Place Names of New Mexico*. Albuquerque, N.M.: University of New Mexico Press, 1998.

Patterson, David. *Alternative Routes from Mexico to Canada for the Continental Divide Trail*. Redstone, Colo.: White Root Press, 1999.

Pern, Stephen. *The Great Divide: A Walk Through America Along the Continental Divide*. New York: Viking Penguin Inc., 1988.

Robbins, Michael, and Paul Chesley. *High Country Trail: Along the Continental Divide*. Washington, D.C.: National Geographic Society, 1981.

Smith, Scott T. *Along Wyoming's Continental Divide Trail*. Englewood, Colo.: Westcliffe Publishers, 2000.

APPENDIX B
Trail Advocacy Groups

American Long Distance Hikers Association–West (ALDHA–West): Promotes fellowship among long-distance hikers by holding a gathering and publishing the *Distance Hiker's Gazette*. ALDHA–West, P.O. Box 5286, Eugene, OR 97405; website: www.gorp.com/nonprof/aldhaw/.

Appalachian Long Distance Hikers Association (ALDHA): Promotes the interests of the long-distance hiking community primarily on trails in the East, but also on long-distance trails anywhere in the world. ALDHA, 10 Benning St. PMB 224, West Lebanon, NH 03784; website: www.aldha.org.

Continental Divide Trail Alliance (CDTA): A nonprofit organization dedicated to helping federal land managers complete, manage, and preserve the trail. CDTA, P.O. Box 628, Pine, CO 80470; phone: (888) 909-CDTA; e-mail: CDNST@aol.com; website: www.cdtrail.org.

Continental Divide Trail Society (CDTS): This grass-roots organization participates in the planning, development, and maintenance of the trail. CDTS, 3704 N. Charles St. #601, Baltimore, MD 21218-2300; phone: (410) 235-9610; e-mail: cdtsociety@aol.com; website: www.gorp.com/cdts/.

Leave No Trace: This group promotes low-impact wilderness travel. Leave No Trace, P.O. Box 997, Boulder, CO 80305; phone: (800) 332-4100; website: www.lnt.org.

Anasazi petroglyphs stand the test of time in El Malpais National Conservation Area.

HISTORY OF THE CONTINENTAL DIVIDE NATIONAL SCENIC TRAIL

The Continental Divide National Scenic Trail (CDNST) began in 1966 as the dream of Benton MacKaye, an 87-year-old man who had already devoted much of his life to seeing the Appalachian Trail come to fruition. MacKaye's idea was to create a trail that would connect a series of wilderness areas along the Divide from Montana's border with Canada to New Mexico's border with Mexico.

MacKaye (rhymes with "deny") proposed his idea to Congress, which soon authorized a study of the trail under the National Trails Act of 1968. At around the same time, a Baltimore attorney by the name of Jim Wolf was hiking the 2,000-mile-long Appalachian Trail, which he completed in 1971. Inspired to seek out a new hiking challenge further afield, Wolf walked the Divide Trail from the Canadian border to Rogers Pass, Montana, in 1973. He soon published a guidebook covering that section of the trail and devoted much of his time to advocating its official designation. After a 1976 study by the Bureau of Outdoor Recreation found the scenic quality of the trail to surpass anything available anywhere else in the country, the Congressional Oversight Committee of the National Trail System held hearings on the trail in 1978, at which Wolf testified. The CDNST received official recognition from Congress later that year under the National Parks and Recreation Act.

In that same year, Wolf founded the Continental Divide Trail Society (CDTS) to garner publicity for the trail and involve the public in work surrounding its construction, particularly its route selection. Wolf continued to hike portions of the trail each summer, and by the mid-'80s he had completed all of its 3,100 miles.

The United States Forest Service is responsible for managing most of the land through which the trail passes. In the 1980s, its work on the trail progressed at different rates in different areas, but it suffered in general from a lack of public involvement. In 1994, two trail advocates began working under the auspices of a group called the Fausel Foundation to raise funds and build support for the trail. By 1995, their efforts evolved into the Continental Divide Trail Alliance (CDTA), a nonprofit organization devoted to fund-raising, publicity, education about the trail, and grass-roots volunteer coordination. The CDTA founders were Bruce Ward, formerly the president of the American Hiking Society, and his wife, Paula, a landscape architect.

In its first year, the CDTA grew to 425 individuals or families, 20 corporate sponsors, and a budget of $400,000. Estimates suggest the Alliance coordinated volunteer work worth $70,000 in that first year. However, trail advocates are quick to point out that there is much work yet to be done. Completion and maintenance of the trail will require funding and volunteer coordination throughout the 21st century.

GENEROUSLY CONTRIBUTED BY TOM LORANG JONES
Revised from *Colorado's Continental Divide Trail: The Official Guide*

The Continental Divide Trail Alliance
Protecting a Vital National Resource

How can you help?
By becoming a member of the Continental Divide Trail Alliance (CDTA). Your willingness to join thousands of concerned citizens across the country will make the difference. Together, we can provide the financial resources needed to complete the trail.

The CDTA is a nonprofit membership organization formed to help protect, build, maintain, and manage the CDT. The CDTA serves a broad-based constituency and includes people who enjoy recreating on public lands, as well as those concerned about overdevelopment.

As a CDTA member, you will:

- Protect a vital and precious natural resource
- Ensure trail maintenance and completion
- Improve trail access
- Support informational and educational programs
- Champion volunteer projects
- Advocate for policy issues that support the CDT

What does it take to help us? Just one cent a mile.
We realize there are a lot of demands on your time and budget. That's why we're only asking you to give a little—just one cent a mile to support the Trail. For a modest membership fee of $31, you will help us go so very far, and finish what was courageously started so long ago.

For more information, or to send your contribution, write to:
Continental Divide Trail Alliance
P.O. Box 628
Pine, CO 80470
(303) 838-3760
www.cdtrail.org
Please make checks payable to CDTA.

Part of the proceeds from the sale of this book benefits the Continental Divide Trail Alliance.

A meadow glows at first light in the San Pedro Parks Wilderness.

PHOTO CREDITS

Front Cover: Tom Till
Page 1: Tom Till
Pages 2-3: William Stone
Page 4: Tom Till
Page 5: David Patterson
Page 6: Tom Till
Page 7: Tom Till
Page 8: Tom Till
Page 9: Tom Till
Page 10: William Stone
Page 11: David Patterson
Page 12: Tom Till
Page 13: Tom Till
Page 14: Tom Till
Page 15: Tom Till
Page 16: Tom Till
Page 17: David Patterson
Page 18: William Stone
Page 19: William Stone
Page 20: Tom Till
Page 21: David Patterson
Page 22: Tom Till
Page 23: Tom Till
Page 24: Tom Till
Page 25: Tom Till
Pages 26-27: Tom Till
Page 28: William Stone
Page 29: William Stone
Page 30: William Stone
Page 31: Tom Till (right) and David Patterson
Page 33: William Stone

A storm passes over El Malpais National Monument.

Page 34: William Stone
Page 35: David Patterson
Page 36: Tom Till
Page 37: William Stone
Page 38: William Stone
Page 39: Tom Till
Page 40: Tom Till
Page 41: William Stone

Pages 42-43: William Stone
Page 44: William Stone
Page 45: Tom Till (both)
Pages 46-47: William Stone
Page 48: Tom Till
Page 49: David Patterson
Page 50: Tom Till
Page 51: Tom Till

Pages 52-53: William Stone
Page 54: Tom Till
Page 55: Tom Till
Page 56: Tom Till
Page 57: Tom Till
Page 58: William Stone
Page 59: Tom Till
Page 60: Tom Till
Page 61: Tom Till
Pages 62-63: William Stone
Page 64: Tom Till
Page 65: David Patterson
Page 66: Tom Till
Page 67: William Stone
Pages 68-69: William Stone
Page 70: William Stone
Page 71: Tom Till
Page 72: Tom Till
Page 73: Tom Till
Pages 74-75: William Stone
Page 76: Tom Till
Page 77: Tom Till
Page 78: Tom Till (both)
Page 79: Tom Till
Page 80: William Stone
Page 81: William Stone
Page 83: William Stone
Page 85: William Stone
Page 86: Tom Till
Page 87: William Stone
Page 88: William Stone
Back Cover: Tom Till

AFTERWORD

The view from Sandstone Bluffs Overlook in El Malpais National Monument opens to sandstone cliffs and boulders.

After hiking for six weeks and approximately 800 miles through New Mexico, Karyn left the trail at Cumbres Pass, the Colorado–New Mexico border. From there I continued hiking alone until I met up with a British gentleman, Andrew Helliwell. Andrew and I hiked loosely together most of the way, accompanied for nearly 1,000 miles by another hiker, C. W. Banfield. I completed hiking the entire Continental Divide Trail from Mexico to Canada on October 3, 1998, just before the onset of winter.

There's no trail or mountain range that doesn't pale in comparison to the Continental Divide Trail. Though every place offers a sense of the unique, the CDT—that beguiling route through mountains and meadows, deserts and canyons—presents a challenge unparalleled by any other National Scenic Trail. More than just a backcountry route, the CDT is one of the few places in the lower 48 states where freedom reigns and wilderness abounds—a land where the grizzly remains king and the coyotes still sing.

—David Patterson

Next page: *A layer of snow blankets several volcanic necks, as viewed from the flank of Cabezon Peak.*